Wheels, wings and water

Buses

Chris Oxlade

Raintree

www.raintreepublishers.co.uk

Visit our website to find out more information about **Raintree** books.

To order:

☎ Phone 44 (0) 1865 888112

▤ Send a fax to 44 (0) 1865 314091

💻 Visit the Raintree Bookshop at **www.raintreepublishers.co.uk** to browse our catalogue and order online.

First published in Great Britain by Raintree, Halley Court, Jordan Hill, Oxford OX2 8EJ, part of Harcourt Education.
Raintree is a registered trademark of Harcourt Education Ltd.

Editorial: Charlotte Guillain and Isabel Thomas
Design: Sue Emerson (HL-US) and Joanna Sapwell (www.tipani.co.uk)
Picture Research: Maria Joannou and Su Alexander
Production: Lorraine Hicks

Originated by Dot Gradations
Printed and bound in China by South China Printing Company

ISBN 1 844 21373 0
07 06 05 04 03
10 9 8 7 6 5 4 3 2 1

British Library Cataloguing in Publication Data
Oxlade, Chris
Buses. – (Wheels, wings and water)
1.Buses – Juvenile literature
I.Title
388.3'4233
A full catalogue record for this book is available from the British Library.

Acknowledgements
The publishers would like to thank the following for permission to reproduce photographs:
Collections/ Peter Wright, **14**; Collections/ Ray Roberts, **19**; Collections/ VI, **6**; London Transport Museum, **4**; Trip/ B Turner, **17**; Trip/ Derick Thomas, **10** Trip/ H Rogers, **7**, **9**, **11**, **12**, **13**, **16**, **18**, **21**, **22**; Trip/ P Treanor, **15**;
Tudor Photography, **8**, **20**; Tudor Shooting, **5**.

Cover photograph reproduced with permission of Collections/ VI

Every effort has been made to contact copyright holders of any material reproduced in this book. Any omissions will be rectified in subsequent printings if notice is given to the publishers.

Contents

Some words are shown in bold, **like this**.
They are explained in the glossary on page 23.

What is a bus?

A bus is a **vehicle** that carries lots of people.

This bus is carrying people around a city.

These children are going to school by bus.

People who ride in a bus are called passengers.

What kinds of bus are there?

This is a double-decker bus.
It has two decks.

Some buses only have one deck.

Coaches carry people on
long journeys.

There is a big space for **luggage**
underneath the seats.

What do bus wheels do?

Buses have big wheels.

The wheels let the bus roll along the road.

tyre

Each wheel has a fat **tyre** to stop the bus from slipping on the road.

The tyres make the bus ride less bumpy.

What makes a bus go?

A bus has an **engine** that makes its wheels turn round.

When the wheels turn round, the bus moves along the road.

An engine needs **fuel** to make
it work.

The fuel goes into the fuel tank.

What does a bus driver do?

A bus driver steers the bus left and right.

She also makes it start and stop.

The bus driver collects the **fare** from every passenger.

Where do buses go?

Most buses work in towns and cities.

Each bus follows a route through the streets.

Some busy roads have a bus lane.

Cars are not allowed in the
bus lane.

Where do people get on and off?

People get on and off the bus at a bus stop.

Passengers ring the bell when they want to get off the bus.

Buses start their journeys at a bus station.

These buses are waiting to start their journeys.

What bus runs on rails?

A tram is a bus that runs on rails.

It is like a train that drives on the road.

tramlines

The rails for a tram are called **tramlines**.

Tramlines are buried in the road.

Who looks after buses?

Sometimes buses get dirty.

The bus station has a special bus wash to clean dirty buses.

Some parts of a bus wear out.

A mechanic replaces the old parts with new ones.

Bus map

seat

mirror

route sign

wheel

driver

Glossary

engine
machine that makes a vehicle move by making the wheels turn round

fare
money that a person pays to travel on a bus

fuel
liquid or gas that burns in an engine to make energy

luggage
the things that a person takes with them on a journey

tramlines
metal bars on the ground for the wheels of a tram to go on

tyre
rubber strip on the outside of a wheel

vehicle
machine that carries people or things from place to place

Index

Titles in the Wheels, Wings and Water series include:

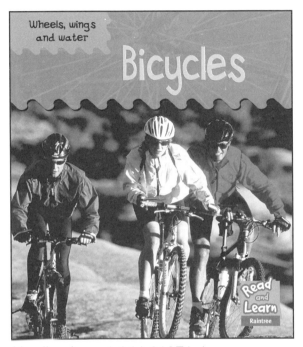

Hardback   1 844 21371 4

Hardback   1 844 21372 2

Hardback   1 844 21373 0

Hardback   1 844 21374 9

Find out about the other titles in this series on our website www.raintreepublishers.co.uk